Quantum Psychology

By: Dr. William D. Horton, Psy. D.

For Information and to contact
William D. Horton, Psy.D.
www.drwillhorton.com
941-468-8551

Table Of Contents

Introduction ....

Chapter 1 There's More To You Than
Meets The Eye ....

Chapter 2 The Power of Symbols..........................

Chapter 3 A New Way Of Thinking.....................

Chapter 4 Balancing Your Energy........................

Chapter 5 The Incredible Power of Beliefs ......

Chapter 6 The Power of Intention ....

Chapter 7 Neuro-Linguistic Programming
(NLP) and Hypnosis..

Chapter 8 Using Your Values as a Driving
Force for Change ....

Chapter 9 Working Within the Logical
Levels of Change..

Chapter 10 Connecting With Others..................

Introduction

Gandhi believed that "A man is but the product of his thoughts. What he thinks, he becomes." Some cultures embrace the concept that each of us was born into this world with a fate or destiny and others are convinced that nothing has been preordained and life is what we make it. Then there is another school of thought that believes that the truth is somewhere in the middle and that each of us is born with a purpose in this life, but whether or not we live that purpose is up to us.

The more scientists research life and the components that create life, the more information and theories exist; but no matter what the theories or modality are, somewhere in the midst of them is the reality that our thoughts and emotions are at the helm of our lives. As the saying goes, life is 10 percent about what happens to you and 90 percent about what you do with it. And the power in that 90 percent resides within our thoughts and perceptions.

For example, some people who get a diagnosis of a disease such as cancer will see it as a death sentence whereas others will see it as a challenge and an opportunity. In each case, it is the person's thoughts and perceptions around the situation that will create the course of action and the outcome.

It seems as though there is a constant stream of new philosophies to help us understand how to live our lives. Yet changing any aspect of our life always comes down to the basic concept that in order to create any alteration in our lives we have to change our mind from its current thought process to a new one—whether the modality we use is traditional therapy that deals with past experiences and helps us put a new perspective around those occurrences or whether it is the law of attraction that requires us to pay attention to our emotions and the thoughts behind those emotions. In other words, no matter what modality of change we are looking at, it all comes down to our thoughts, emotions and choices.

But what are thoughts? Where do they come from? Do they all originate somewhere in our own minds or do they come from "the space beyond the mind?"

Science has taught us a lot about the human mind and how it works, and quantum physics has opened up our understanding of the universe and its impact on us as individuals. By combining the knowledge we have available of ourselves as individuals and of the universe as a whole, we can get a better understanding of where our thoughts come from and how we can assert more control over what we think, which will ultimately affect how we feel, thus impacting our life in general.

This book is about understanding the power in who we are as human beings along with the tools and information that we all have available to us. With this knowledge, we can learn to control of our thoughts, emotions and perceptions and use them in helping us make decisions that will ensure the outcomes we desire.

With the basics of quantum physics, which is the science of possibilities, and the knowledge about ourselves that is available to us within the context of numerology, along with the tools of neuro-linguistic programming and hypnosis, each one of us can use the power of intention to create a life that is filled with health, happiness and success.

Chapter 1

There's More To You Than Meets The Eye

When you reach the end of what you should know, you will be
at the beginning of what you should sense.
~Kahlil Gibran

What Are You Exactly?

When you look in the mirror, you see a person with all of the external details that are a part of any human being. But are you really what you see in the mirror? Think about it for a minute...you also have thoughts, feelings and emotions, yet you can't see them.

While part of you appears to be a solid mass, there is also a part of you that is intangible. Where does the intangible part come from? Does it comes from the part you see in the mirror, or does the form you see in the mirror actually come from the thoughts, feelings and emotions you can't see? And, is the body you see in the mirror really a solid mass in the first place?

According to quantum physics, all solid objects (including human beings) are actually tiny bits of matter or energy surrounded by vast fields of empty space. In other words, what appears to be solid and real, when looked at from its tiniest levels, is something totally different. In fact, at our very tiniest levels, human beings are indistinguishable from any other piece of the universe. Everything in the universe (from the chair you sit on to the computer you work on to the car you drive to the heart that beats inside of you) is made up of teeny tiny bands of vibrating energy surrounded by vast, empty spaces of nothingness. It is the frequency at which these bands of energy vibrate that largely determines what form energy will take.

The solidity that we perceive, it seems, is an illusion. And yet, when you place your mostly empty-space hand on your mostly empty-space keyboard, what do you feel? Certainly not empty space. Instead, you feel solid matter connecting with other solid matter. Your hand doesn't pass right through the keyboard like you might think it would given both are mostly empty spaces. But why not?

The answer lies in energy fields. While it is a fact that the universe is made up of mostly empty space, energy fields exist between particles that allow you to perceive that which is mostly empty space as a solid object. It's a pretty cool magic trick. These fields of energy hold everything together and give us the illusion of solidity to such a degree that nearly everyone in the world has firmly bought into the belief that all we see around us is solid and real.

Yet matter is a tricky thing because apparently all we perceive as real in this universe is really something different than it appears. Empty space is a part of it, but there's more. Even as we are thinking about matter as particles surrounded by vast empty spaces, we're not getting the whole idea. That's because even those "solid" particles that make up matter aren't really solid. At least not always.

Experiments in quantum physics have been performed that demonstrate something called wave/particle duality. Through an experiment known as the double slit experiment, it has been demonstrated that all of the particles making up matter exist simultaneously as both a wave and a particle. In other words, each particle is either energy (wave) or mass (particle). Matter doesn't only exist as matter; it also exists as energy. These two things exist in a state of what is known as "quantum superposition." That is, it exists in a state where it is neither a wave nor a particle, but rather as the possibility of both until it is either observed or measured.

In the moment that it is observed or measured, then the quantum superposition is resolved by "wave function collapse." And then what once existed as a possibility of one or more states now exists in a single state because it has been observed. Had there been no observer, then the wave/particle would have existed infinitely in a state of pure possibility. It is true that a brick wall looks and feels real and it leaves bruises when you smack into it, but it was your interaction with it (as the observer) that brought it into solidity.

This is the basis of our entire universe. If it happens on a miniscule level with every single particle that makes up the matter of our solid universe, then it logically follows that the universal rules that apply to the tiny bits of structure underlying everything in the universe also apply to things on a large scale. Since the macro is made up of the micro, then it is only logical that if things behave in such a way on a micro scale, they must also behave that way on a macro scale.

Changing Forms

It gets even more interesting because something that may appear one way under a certain set of circumstances may react or look another way under another set of circumstances. A good example of what I mean by this statement is a science class experiment with a substance called oobleck.

Oobleck is a simple mixture of cornstarch and water, which makes it a liquid...right? Well, it is...that is until pressure is applied and then it becomes a solid. And when it is subjected to vibration and pressure it can seem almost supernatural in its antics with waves and droplets coming off of what appears to be a solid sheet. This same complexity that exists within the simple mixture of cornstarch and water exists within a human being as well. We are solid, yet like all of the matter around us, we are made up of tiny vibrating bands of energy surrounded by vast, empty spaces. And when we interact and collide with other people or substances, there is an exchange of matter which affects everyone and everything involved.

It is because of this exchange of matter that forensic science often helps law enforcement "get their man." Because we interact physically we all leave traces of ourselves wherever we have been and at the same time, we pick up traces of where we have been and carry them with us...in reality changing both us and "where we have been." In quantum physics, this exchange is referred to as quantum entanglement.

Quantum Entanglement

Simply put, the theory of quantum entanglement (a.k.a. "spooky action at a distance," which has borne out experimentally in mathematics and in the laboratory), states that whenever a pair of subatomic particles has interaction, they become forever entangled with one another. And once entanglement occurs, those two particles are forever linked, which means that whatever affects one of the pair of particles will affect the other. Time, distance and space between the particles doesn't matter in the slightest. When one particle is affected, the other is instantaneously affected as well.

In fact, what is known in the scientific world as "The Big Bang" was basically particle interaction which resulted in quantum entanglement that theoretically connected every sub-atomic particle in the universe with every other sub-atomic particle in the universe in a web of interlinked particles. In other words, no matter where each particle exists in space or time, those links remain in place, which means that information received by one particle is instantaneously received by every other particle in the entire universe. In the scientific realm, this interconnected web in referred or as "the zero point field" or "the scalar field." In New Age circles, this web is called "the collective consciousness."

This zero point field or collective consciousness offers up a potential explanation for why you or your partner have the same thought at exactly the same moment. Because our bodies and our minds are made up of these entangled sub-atomic particles that receive and respond to information instantaneously, circumstances such as these may actually be the sub-atomic particles of both your mind and that of your partner's receiving the same information instantaneously. This theory can also explain why your mood may be affected by a happy person in a room (or the cranky one) in spite of the fact that you haven't interacted with either of them. In actuality, it is one giant, entangled universe that responds as a single organism to applied stimulus.

This stimulus can, however, be more than what we perceive as physical. It can be any energy form, including: thought, prayer, emotion and belief. In fact, there have been studies that show that thought forms of energy (such as prayer) can travel backwards through time to affect a physical organism. And positive things can happen because of this collective consciousness. Society as a whole can change because as each one of us changes, we can positively affect the whole.

Our Personal Filters

However, the question becomes...why aren't we all affected by everything that happens if we are all connected in quantum entanglement? The explanation lies in filtering. In order to survive, humans have become very adept at putting filters in place in order to shift through all of the information that bombards us on every level. Without these filters, we would be constantly inundated with so much information that we would barely be able to function. Therefore, we have subconsciously learned to sift through information so that we experience only those bits of data that we find relevant to our own personal points of view.

The good news is that you do not need to be affected by the negative energy of other people. When such a negative energy transfer occurs, most people are unaware of what has happened and they assume that what they are experiencing is their own "mood." But by being aware of the process by which these interactions occur, and by providing yourself with the appropriate tools to counteract such interactions, you can create a life that brings you the health and happiness you desire and positively impact each moment in your life to work toward that end result.

While quantum physics and its theories have been around since the middle of the twentieth century, its applications into our everyday life are just now being explored. People are discovering that the laws of quantum physics may be able to be applied on a personal level in ways that positively affect our behavior, psychology, health, and indeed, the very fabric of our lives.

The Truth About Energy

Using the word "energy" often has 'woo woo' New Age connotations, but the energetic structure that underlies our very universe also has a basis in science. As previously discussed, everything and everyone that exists is made up of the same stuff: teeny tiny particles that all behave in the same way until they are measured or observed, then they become one or the other—a particle or a wave. Therefore, until the observer comes into the picture, each unit that makes up solid matter exists only as the possibility to be mass or energy.

If one truly understands this—that everything exists in a state of possibility until it is observed—then it has some pretty earth-shattering implications. It means that there is nothing but possibility until an observer enters the picture. Only in that moment do the tiniest units of matter pull together to form something solid or something energetic.

The phrase, "everything in the universe," covers a lot of ground. Look around you at all of the solid objects you see— the trees, the sky, your desk, a credenza, a chair, your arm— but those things are only a small part of "everything" in the universe. In this case, the word "everything" is truly all-inclusive. Not only does it consist of *tangibles* like grass, plants and animals, but it also consists of *intangibles* like thought, belief, visualization and emotion.

Each of these intangibles is made up of the very same stuff of which tangibles are made. However, because you don't experience them with your five senses, it is difficult to realize that something such as a thought has a physical basis.

It does. Thought reaches into that realm where everything exists as pure possibility—the quantum ooze where micro particles await an observer to settle into a final state. Thought extracts some of those particles from that state of possibility, and they become energy. As we have shown, energy is not merely energy, it contains the possibility of becoming something solid and tangible. It can become a *thing.*In a very real way, thoughts can and do become things under the right set of circumstances.

Albert Einstein demonstrated that matter and energy are essentially the same thing ($E=mc^2$). And *The Law of Conservation of Energy* tells us that energy can neither be created nor destroyed—it can only change forms. Both thoughts and emotions are energetic forms. Mass and energy are the same thing, and all energy is entangled (connected). So it makes sense that the energy from a thought or emotion can become a physical reaction.

If thoughts (energy) can become physical (matter), then it stands to reason that controlling our thoughts may just allow us to shape our experiences in life. So, although you can look in the mirror and see the external aspects of who you are, you are not seeing all of who you are. It is the parts of you that you cannot see with the naked eye (your thoughts and your emotions) that can have the biggest impact on the health and happiness that you experience in your life.

Through the science of quantum physics we come to understand that a person's future is changed, defined and fine-tuned by their own thoughts (or vibrations) and what they pull into the field of existence.

So when you look in the mirror and you see the external details of your physical being, remember, there is so much more to you (and everything around you) than what meets the   eye.

Chapter 2

The Power of Symbols

What we think determines what happens to us,
so if we want to change our lives,
we need to stretch our minds.
~Wayne Dyer

Understanding ourselves is just part of the equation for a healthy, happy life. Successfully interacting with others in all areas of our lives is a crucial component as well. And this type of interaction requires knowing and understanding others, which is accomplished through communication.

Communication is an essential part of every facet of our lives and can often be a deciding factor in the success or failure of our relationships or careers. While it is important to learn to express ourselves through words, they are actually only a part of how we relate to and express ourselves with each other.

In fact, for as long as human beings have communicated, symbols have been a part of that interaction, used for everything from religious practices to science and mathematics. Even before the written word, verbal symbols were used to signify objects and concepts. Then as language evolved into written words, those verbal signs were translated first into pictograms and then later into words spelled out according to the sounds that make up the word.

A symbol is something that represents something else, and they are much more than those things you see above your number keys on your computer keyboard. Symbols can also be gestures, pictures, words, objects, markings or even sounds.

Early pictograms (or drawings) provided a representation of the stories, beliefs, daily lives and history of those who used them. As a matter of fact, while there may have been history that occurred before the onset of the written language, our knowledge of history begins with the rudimentary early symbolic attempts at the written language.

In the rudimentary beginnings of the written word, the use of symbols was necessary for maintaining history, sharing information, keeping financial information and much more. It is believed that the use of writing systems as a cultural form of symbology began somewhere around the third millennium BCE. Symbols have been around a very long time! Even Stone Age man left behind drawings or carvings—mostly of animals—on a number of mediums including bone and ivory. These symbols left by prehistoric man give us insight into what was important to them, yet very few of the symbols they used tell us of their history.

Just as the meaning of a word can sometimes change over the course of history, so is the case with some symbols. The swastika is a perfect example. Swastika symbols have been found as far back as 1000 BCE and for thousands of years it was used by countries and cultures such as China, England, Greece and India to denote positive meanings such as sun, power, strength and luck. It was also used in worship in various religious practices. In fact Buddhism and Hinduism still commonly use the swastika as a religious symbol.

However, in the 1800's, German nationalists began to use the swastika to represent German/Aryian history and in 1920, Hitler co-opted the use of the swastika as the official symbol of the Nazi party. Because of Hitler's political beliefs, this symbol that represented positive ideas and feelings for thousands of years became the symbol of anti-Semitism, hate, murder and suffering.

Symbols and Psychology

Since a symbol is a representation of something else, when we experience any type of symbol, we filter it through perceptions, belief systems, knowledge, agendas and more. For instance, when you see the swastika, what is your reaction? Is it a negative one or a positive one? Your personal experiences, psychology, knowledge, history and beliefs all blend together to form your perception of a symbol when you see it. Chances are that when you see a swastika, your reactions are instantaneous and strong. You don't stop to consciously consider what that symbol means to you and what you know of it. Instead, you very likely process it instantly and immediately have a gut-level reaction to it.

That is the power of all symbols. They can instantaneously evoke tremendous emotion and exert psychological influence without any conscious thought. We are impacted by and respond to symbols every day of our lives without having to put any thought into our reactions or responses—they spring up from our subconscious which houses all of our preprogrammed perceptions.

The following story provides an example of the power of symbols or symbolic gestures in communicating thoughts and emotions:

Suppose you are driving down the freeway in heavy, bumper-to-bumper traffic. Your car's movement is stop-and-go at best, and as is typical in that type of traffic, everyone is trying to change lanes and get into the lane that they perceive is moving the fastest. You notice a car on your right trying to edge into your lane. It has its turn signal on and the driver is giving you "the look." You're in a pretty good mood, so you hold your position for a moment to let the driver pull in front of you to get into your lane. You may even toss him (or her) a little wave to let him know he can proceed. Through his back window, you see the driver give you a little wave.

Then you hear a loud honk come from the car behind you. Looking in your rear-view mirror, you see the driver in that car giving you another type of gesture altogether.

While the above scenario can be a pretty normal, everyday occurrence, it is rife with symbols, all of which evoked certain responses in you, given your psychological presets and filters.

The first symbols you noticed were the flickering turn signal and "the look" from the driver to your right. Depending on your mood, your level of politeness, how you interpreted that driver's behavior, your belief about how you should treat others, along with a number of other factors, you instantaneously decided how to react to his symbols, and you reacted accordingly. You then sent out a symbol of your own by resting your foot on your brakes for a moment and waving to the driver that it was okay to get in front of you. Like you, the driver immediately reacted given his psychological filters and presets. Then he provided you with a symbol of his own—the courtesy wave—which you no doubt interpreted as a "thank you," and your reaction was either a neutral or a happy one, depending on your psychological state.

Alas, the driver behind you then decided to send you a few signals of his (or her) own. The first was the honk, and then the gesture. How you responded to those signals again rested on your psychological presets. While one person might merely laugh and wave, another might return the gesture. This is the reason why some traffic incidents evolve into road rage and other don't.

Let's look at another symbolic situation involving body language:

Ned is a pretty shy guy who has never had a lot of luck with women. So his friend Dave decides to take him out to a dance club and show him a thing or two about landing the ladies. As you may have already guessed, Dave considers himself a "ladies' man." Once at the club, Ned and Dave are standing at the bar when they spot a pretty woman who seems to be looking at them in the mirror at the back of the bar. She looks up, smiles and runs a hand across her mouth.

"Oh my God," Ned thinks. "I've got something on my face!" He quickly and surreptitiously begins to wipe his mouth to remove whatever is there so that the woman will stop laughing at him.

"Allllllll rightttt," Dave thinks. "She's really digging me." He straightens himself to his full height and primps.

The woman at the bar? It doesn't really matter what she intended, or if she was even communicating symbolically with either Dave or Ned. She could have seen her reflection in the mirror and noticed her lipstick was too bright. Each person is interpreting the symbols based upon their own filters.

We each have our own personal reactions many times a day to a variety of symbols and gestures. Some of our responses are programmed by society. For instance, when you are driving and you see an octagon-shaped sign that is red in color, you bring your vehicle to a halt. Much of time, we are not even aware of our precepts or reactions to symbols or symbolic gestures. Those precepts of common symbols or symbolic gestures can often differ from those of people around us, not only because of our personal experiences, but sometimes because of the culture in which we live or were raised.

Common Symbols

The following are some of the common symbols that are often used by many people on a daily basis and the typical meanings that are attached to these symbols.

Symbol	Meaning
Thumbs up gesture	In the U.S., it means "all right; right on; good job."
	In many Eastern and African cultures, it is a pejorative, "up yours."

	In Iraq, Iran, Thailand and Bangladesh, it is an obscene gesture similar to the middle finger gesture in the U.S.
	In the UK, it is a greeting or recognition.
$	This symbol represents currency in the U.S., Australia, Mexico and other countries around the world.
	This is the symbol for currency in some European countries.
	A religious symbol most commonly representing the cross on which Jesus died.
	This symbol is used worldwide to mean "no smoking."

Symbols and the Subconscious

The truth is that the way you interpret and respond to any type of symbol relies entirely on what you have learned and how you have been subconsciously programmed. For instance, a simple symbol such as a dollar sign ($) may trigger two entirely different responses in two different people.

In one person, the symbol may trigger feelings of guilt, anger and despair because they have struggled all of their lives with money, don't pay their bills, or were raised truly believing that money is the root of all evil. In another person, the same symbol may trigger feelings of joy or ambition or power. Again, it all depends on the subconscious learning that has taken place.

The Use of Subconscious Symbols in Advertising

Advertisers know and understand how easy it is to manipulate the subconscious mind of potential customers by using symbols in images, logos, words, etc. Papers have been written and studies performed showing how easy it is to induce certain desirable populations to buy products by using symbols that target the psyche of those populations.

For instance, an ad for a product targeting Christians may feature subtle crosses, and merchandise targeting the same audience is often arranged in cross shapes. Or if the target is a young, hip audience, a phallic symbol might be hidden in the advertisement in the form of a neck tie, a tube of lipstick or a monument. This type of advertising is referred to as subliminal seduction, and it works. By camouflaging any number of symbols in their ads, advertisers have long been able to elicit a certain response from a desired segment of the public.

Using Symbols as a Tool for Change

Since we subconsciously respond to symbols without forethought, we can use that power of instantaneous reaction to change our lives.

For instance, NLP uses symbols or symbolic gestures to anchor thought patterns or behaviors, thus "reprogramming" the subconscious mind with a different response—typically for changing negative reactions to positive ones. (NLP will be discussed in more detail toward the end of this book.)

Chapter 3

A New Way of Thinking

When we direct our thoughts properly,
we can control our emotions.
~W. Clement Stone

Just as mankind has evolved throughout the years, so too has the way that we perceive the effect that our minds and our thoughts have on our lives. With more and more research indicating that our thoughts can turn into matter (emotions) which impacts our reactions and choices, thus creating our reality, a new approach was born that lends insight into how we view and deal with our thoughts. This new approach is called quantum psychology.

What is Quantum Psychology?

It is simply the application of the logic of quantum physics—currently the most accurate and mathematically precise model we have of our sub-atomic universe—to the field of psychology. As we discussed in the beginning of this book, quantum physics teaches us that everything around us exists in a state of pure possibility until we, as observers, interact with it. Everything we know and experience is made up of tiny particles—not just matter, but also our thoughts, words and actions.

Thoughts arise as the result of a physical and energetic process. They arise from the quantum soup that exists as pure possibility. Without physical and energetic matter, there would be no thought. The physical basis of thought is a scientific fact. It is derived from the firing of neurons and synapses that generate brain waves. Once a thought has formed, it has an energetic process all its own. It now exists as its own energetic parcel out in the universe, separate from the body, yet still connected to you through teeny tiny energy channels that hold the entire universe together.

As early as 391 BC, Plato postulated the law of affinity—that 'like tends towards like.' Since then, many scientists have worked with the laws of attraction, which current quantum theory models now call field particle exchange. It is these laws of attraction where quantum physics can have psychological application that can change the course of your life.

In the last few years a lot has been written about the law of attraction and how a person can use it to change their life simply by changing their thoughts. However, without the scientific understanding of how thoughts are created and thus changed, the law of attraction, while plausible and understandable, sometimes seems unattainable. Being able to control the thoughts that are "sending out the messages to the universe" that are attracting "other like matter" can often feel like a gargantuan and impossible task.

That's where quantum psychology enters the picture. It has much to teach us about the inner workings of our mind and how we can use that knowledge to change our thoughts, and in doing so, change our minds to create the life we want.

The Power of Thoughts and Perceptions

According to quantum psychology, your thoughts and perceptions have a huge effect on your experience of the world. In fact, negative thought patterns can and do affect everything in your life from your health and wellness to your prosperity and happiness. The reason behind this is that research is proving that thoughts do actually become reality.

Some of the most interesting research into the power of words and thoughts was done by Japanese researcher Dr. Masaru Emoto[2] who experimentally showed how different thoughts affected the formation of untreated, distilled water crystals. Emoto filled several glass bottles with water and then taped a different message to several of the bottles. He also subjected some of the bottles of water to different types of music—from heavy metal to classical—and then all of the bottles of water were frozen and the crystals were photographed.

The messages that Emoto taped to some of the bottles of water varied from "You make me sick, I will kill you," to "Mother Teresa," and from "Love and Appreciation," to "Thank You," and "Adolph Hitler." Although the water in the bottles came from the same source, were in exactly the same types of glass containers and were frozen in the same manner, the crystals all appeared very different from one another. Those with negative messages taped to the bottle appeared to have failed to form a crystalline structure at all, while those with positive messages formed beautiful, symmetrical crystals, much like a snowflake. And the pattern followed through in the same way for the water that was subjected to music. The heavy metal music water had no crystal formation while the water that was exposed to peaceful music had beautiful, symmetrical crystals. Emoto's conclusion from his research is that thoughts and consciousness do have an effect on your environment.

Emoto's research raises some very interesting questions. If words and sounds can have that kind of impact on water, imagine the impact that those same things have on a human being. And words, thoughts and experiences are happening to all of us each moment of every day, both consciously and unconsciously.

Both quantum psychology and traditional psychology have shown that thoughts and beliefs do have an impact on the experiences and outcomes of life. In fact, unless you have consciously reviewed all of your thought patterns and words that were spoken by you or to you, thoughts that you had years ago can still be powerfully impacting you today. Think about it...what were some of the labels that you were given as a child? Are you still unconsciously living out those labels today in your adult life without even realizing it?

Changing Our Thoughts

The exciting thing about the knowledge that has been gained through quantum psychology is that we now know that we can each consciously begin to change our thoughts, and in doing so can change our lives. It is interesting that many of us are impressed by computer technology and what it allows us to do, yet we all have our own built-in computer in the form of the remarkable thing we call our mind. Without putting any conscious effort into it, our minds are continuously performing important tasks like thinking, feeling, remembering, calculating, analyzing and reasoning...to name just a few. And while all of this is going on, we're also cooking a meal or running a business meeting or driving a car or rocking a baby. And the list goes on. By controlling our thoughts so that we are consciously aware of what is going on in our mind, we can take power and responsibility for our own state of mind and the way we interact and communicate.

According to quantum psychology, our experience is mainly a result of our perceptions. How we perceive the world is a direct result of a number of factors including psycho-social programming, experiences and imprinting. The tricky thing about all of this is that the majority of this programming that impacts our perception of the world is happening on a subconscious level and often occurs so instantaneously that we don't even know it's happening. In fact, much of the basis for each of our current belief systems probably happened many years ago, and we are perhaps still reacting in ways that are not necessarily in agreement to what we truly believe now.

It's no secret that we all experience the universe from our own unique point of view. In fact, two people having the very same experience always have different stories to tell about that experience. For instance, eyewitnesses of the same accident will all see something slightly different. The reason behind this phenomena is that each of us as individuals has filters in place that affect our observation of everything that happens in our own personal universe.

The Observer Effect

It is because of these filters that everybody seems to have their own point of view, and getting two people to agree to the same viewpoint can sometimes be a challenge. Quantum psychology is a new way of looking at the human mind that applies the logic of quantum physics. One of the theories in quantum physics that was discussed earlier in this book was the "observer effect," or simply stated, "the observer affects the outcome."

In essence, the observer becomes part of the equation and can't help but interfere merely by attempting to observe or measure something. There is a famous thought experiment in quantum physics known as "Schroedinger's Cat," which explains this duality. According to the thought experiment, a cat is placed in a box with a Geiger counter, a small amount of radioisotope that has a 50% probability of decaying, and a small flask of hydrocyanic acid. If the radioisotope decays, the Geiger counter measures the decay, releasing a small hammer, which breaks the flask and releases the acid. Once the acid is released, the cat dies.

Since the box is closed, the observer would have no way of knowing whether or not the cat was dead or alive until he opened the box and "observed" either a live cat or a dead cat. In the meantime, according to Schroedinger (the author of this thought experiment), the cat existed for the observer in both the alive and dead state until the box was opened and the cat was observed. In other words, the cat existed in neither a state of "yes" or "no," but rather as a "maybe" until the observer took a look and rendered the cat either dead or alive.

If this sounds very much to you like the age old question, "If a tree falls in the woods and no one's around, is there a sound?" You are correct. Both rely on the same principle—that the observer is extremely important in the observation of the universe. In other words, how we "observe" or perceive our universe determines to a large degree what occurs in our universe. Our personal filters have a lot to do with our observations and perceptions.

Our Personal Filters

Our personal filters are an important part of who we are. Without them, we would be continuously bombarded by so much information that we would not be able to fully process our experiences. In other words, our filters are in place as a protective mechanism. Just like our fingerprints are all different, so too are our filtering systems. Each one of us develops our own personal filtering system throughout our lifetime through a variety of types of conditioning, including the symbols and semantics we use for communication, the imprinting we received during our childhood, our life experiences, and even our psychological programming.

Filters in themselves are good because they help us develop and maintain our individuality and our own unique view of the world. No two human beings have the exact same filters in place. These filters (in other words, programming) allow us to define ourselves and form our own judgments and definitions about everything in the world around us. While this all leads to each of us having our own unique view of the world, it also serves to help us maintain our sense of separateness from everyone else. This programming is what allows us to define ourselves as "I" and to determine the "isness" of everything else we encounter.

While our filters can be very positive in our journey to self-definition, they can also be our greatest impediments to discovering who we truly are and in developing a sense of connectedness to the universe. The reason behind this is because our view of ourselves is often far more limited than we actually are. It's like trying to use a globe to represent planet Earth. It gives us a sense of what our world is like, but it is just a small representation of something that is much larger and much more encompassing.

According to the principles of quantum psychology, these limited models of one another and ourselves that we carry around inside of our heads are a source of much of the difficulty we have with interacting as human beings. Indeed, so different are our models of the universe that it is quite possible that no two people have ever truly met. How could they when they each see the world only from their own point of view? From there, it's easy to extrapolate why it is so darn difficult to get others to see things from your point of view. It's because they can't. They simply aren't wired that way. It's actually amazing that we get along as well as we do.

Changing Our Filters and Perceptions

If our point of view is so firmly entrenched, then how can we stop limiting ourselves and our perceptions of others? The answer is by bypassing the filters of others (or your own filters) to establish rapport with another. Once rapport has been established, it becomes easy to anchor certain thoughts, beliefs, emotions and behaviors that can be triggered though simple physical actions.

If it is true that thoughts (energy) can become physical (matter), then it stands to reason that controlling our thoughts (or changing them) may just allow us to shape our experiences in life as well as help us build rapport with others, which will help in developing relationships...from personal to business.

It is certainly true that we are conditioned to see the world in a certain manner; however, this construct that was designed to protect us doesn't need to become self-limiting. Using the knowledge gleaned from quantum psychology along with therapeutic modalities such as hypnosis and NLP, which are covered in detail in Chapter 8 of this book, you can truly change how you see the world.

Dwelling on a negative thought could result in a negative physical outcome, and dwelling on a positive thought could result in a positive physical outcome. However, while it seems well and good to spread a "think positive" message, we all know that there are many times when it feels as if those negative thoughts arise unbidden, and we can't make them go away or replace them with positive thoughts no matter how hard we try. Yet, by understanding how our minds work, we can learn how to reprogram our thought patterns to work in conjunction with the desires we have for our lives.

Understanding Our Minds

Until the last decade, the prevailing scientific theory of neurology was that the human brain could not establish new neural connections. Simply stated, what you are born with is what you have and, as you age, those neurons will die. However, it is now known that the more than one hundred billion neurons of the brain are geared to reinvest in themselves. Positive, enriched environments stimulate the brain to create more neural connections. In other words, the more you learn, the more you become capable of learning. You can actually rewire (reprogram) your brain. And you can do this at any age, because the more you stimulate it, the more it grows. By understanding the capabilities of the conscious and subconscious mind you will be able to make choices that can help you maximize the potential of your mind in all areas of your life.

Your conscious mind is your thinking, awake state of awareness, yet it comprises a remarkably paltry 12 percent of your mind. Your conscious mind has five basic functions:

1. Analysis
2. Rationalization
3. Willpower
4. Functional memory
5. Voluntary body functions

Whereas your subconscious mind that takes up the other 88 percent is the power center—the motherboard of your body. And, just like with a computer—as long as it's working properly, you are not even aware that this part of your mind is even there. However, if it wasn't there and functioning, nothing else could happen...it literally runs your life without you knowing it. The problem is that many people spend too much time listening to that loud, obnoxious 12 percent instead of tapping into their true power center. Like an iceberg, the subconscious mind is hidden with only a small part showing and with a powerful chunk of its entirety sitting just below the surface.

While some of the modalities of change present the possibility of reprogramming our subconscious as a huge, mystical secret that takes years of patience to master, in reality, it is just a matter of knowing the way to activate that powerful 88 percent of your mind. In order to do that, it helps to know what the main functions of your subconscious mind are:

1. It cannot think, reason or argue—it simply FEELS.
2. It is the emotional center of your being.
3. It controls who you are, how you respond and what you believe.
4. Your habits are a function of your subconscious mind.
5. Your subconscious mind protects you from real and imagined dangers.

Your conscious mind is the active master that thinks, perceives, exerts will, is aware, instigates activity and can be objective. Your subconscious mind acts like a servant, yet is really the source of who you are because it controls your feelings, blindly records your experiences and thoughts, is the source of your personal power and is totally subjective. By deliberately using your subconscious mind by allowing suggestions to travel from your conscious to your subconscious mind, you have the power to change your beliefs and behaviors.

Although the field of quantum psychology is a relatively recent innovation, it is revolutionizing the way that many people live their lives. Its principles, based on the sound logic of quantum physics, can be applied to your life as well. In doing so, you can change the way that you think, leading to a happier more fulfilled life.

Chapter 4

Balancing Your Energy

You can never teach a man anything. You can only
help him to discover it within himself.
~Galileo Galilei

The Impact of Energy

Think about the times when you have been around someone who gave off a feeling of negative energy. Perhaps you were in a perfectly good mood before encountering this person. After being in their presence for just a few moments, your mood changed for the worse in spite of the fact that you had no negative interactions. Conversely, how about shiny, happy people? Think about an experience when your mood has been uplifted just by being in the presence of a perpetually happy person.

As I talked about in Chapter 1, because of quantum entanglement, we can sometimes experience feelings and energy that have nothing to do with our own thoughts or experiences because our subconscious filters have been set to accept energy that is on the same "frequency" as our own. And the energy and emotion of events can affect us long after we have forgotten that they have happened. For a long time, this has been believed to be a purely psychological transfer and dealt with by traditional psychological modalities such as talk therapy. But what if it wasn't purely psychological? What if the emotion that lingered actually had a physical basis?

The interaction of emotion and the physical world has been well documented. Studies have shown that the emotions of human beings can affect our physical bodies, creating illness or wellness. Other studies into the Noetic sciences have shown the efficacy of prayer in combating illness. If one looks objectively at these phenomena, it leads to the conclusion that there must be some mechanism of interaction between pure thought and physical reality.

By reprogramming our thoughts and balancing our energy, we can reset our filters and have more choice over what we experience thus choosing a "whole new universe" in which we are happier and more positive.

Neuro-linguistic programming (NLP) and hypnosis are two powerful processes that can be used to set your own personal filters in such a manner that you are not adversely affected by the negativity of others. Both modalities are a wonderful adjunct to quantum psychology, allowing you to work with your mind on a subconscious level where all of your filters reside.

The Importance of Balance

Our bodies are very complex. However, like everything else in nature, they are designed to be in balance and operate efficiently. Yet the laws of entropy work at odds with this statis.

What is entropy? It is a law of thermodynamics that states that, in an isolated system, the degree of disorder is always increasing. Fortunately, the human body is not an isolated system. We can introduce elements into this system (our bodies) that counteract the disorder (decay) that is a natural part of entropy. By using materials—such as food, medication and even crystals—to balance vibrational energy, it is possible to bring your body back into balance and prevent the cycle of emotional, physical and mental disorder that leads to emotional pain and physical disease.

In her book, *Anatomy of the Spirit,*[3] medical intuitive Carolyn Myss, Ph.D. describes the body's energetic system and how emotional imbalances can affect the flow of energy, leading to a number of physical, psychological and emotional illnesses.

Myss describes the body's energetic system in terms of chakras (or in the language of Kabbalistic Jewish mysticism, sefirot). Chakras and sefirot are essentially based upon the same principles of energetic flow throughout the human body. In the chakra system, there are seven chakras that run through the body from head to toe, along the body's central column. These chakras correspond with different colors and different emotional and health issues.

In the Kabbalistic system, there are ten sefirot that roughly correspond with the chakras. Emotional, mental and physical issues can cause blockages in different chakras that disturb the flow of energy throughout the body, leading to disease. Likewise, blockages in the body's energy system based in a physical mechanism can lead to emotional and psychological problems. It can become a circular system that leads to a downward spiral of disease and psychological or emotional pain.

Myss isn't the first to make the correlation between energy flow, emotions and physical health. Many traditions of alternative health care—some of them ancient—also acknowledge how disrupted energy (or chi) flow throughout the body can stem from emotional issues and lead to physical, emotional and psychological disease. Many such forms of healing such as traditional Chinese Medicine, Ayurveda, Reiki, and even chiropractic care all aim to remove energy blockages in order to restore the flow of chi throughout the body.

Crystal healing works with energy medicine and takes it a step further by attempting to balance energy blockages through the specific vibrational energy of certain materials (most often crystals, but sometimes metals and other materials as well). In crystal healing, the healing material is placed on or near the body in the area that corresponds to the specific chakra or energy that is blocked. Similarly, color therapy uses the vibration of different colors to remove energy blockages.

Going Beyond Our Bodies

Some traditions go beyond health into our environment. Feng Shui, for instance, deals with creating an environment that successfully directs the flow of chi throughout living and working spaces in order to induce inner and outer harmony.

Changing Our Energy

None of this sounds possible? Remember, we are all just vibrating energy formed into matter, and all energy is affected by everything it comes in contact with. You can't affect one part of the system without affecting the entire system because it is all entangled. Therefore, introducing an element that vibrates with qualities that can positively affect your life may just balance your energies in such a way that you can affect positive changes without being at the mercy of predetermined numerical traits.

With so many different modalities focusing on balancing and maintaining the energy flow throughout the body and the environment, one wonders if there is a scientific basis that supports these modalities.

When looking at our universe from a quantum perspective, it appears that the answer just may be "yes." On our very smallest levels, human beings—and everything in our universe—are really just tiny bits of vibrating energy surrounded by large areas of empty space. As a matter of fact, vibration is what causes the formation of matter.

For example, if you place several grains of sand on a plate and make the plate vibrate, the individual particles of sand will form and reform into different shapes and patterns depending on the frequency of vibration being applied to the plate.

So it is with everything you see and experience in the universe, including your body, your thoughts and your emotions. Different thoughts and emotions have different vibrational frequencies. Negative thoughts and emotions can cause disequilibrium. How? Every time you think or feel something, those thoughts and emotions resonate a frequency around you that causes other things to begin to vibrate at the same frequency. Much like the sand on the plate, these vibrations can lead to physical changes in your body as the vibration causes your subatomic particles to reform in new ways that match the vibrations given off by your emotions. The stronger the thought or feeling, the stronger the vibration and the more that matter (in this case, your body) is affected by the vibration.

The human body is a delicately balanced system. In order to maintain optimal physical, mental and emotional health, your body needs to maintain its optimum operating frequency or to be able to quickly return itself to stasis after an event that changes its vibration. The longer a body is out of balance, and the longer the flow of energy is disrupted, the more severe the disease and the more difficult it becomes to restore balance and energetic flow.

Crystals and other special materials are believed to vibrate at frequencies that can restore your body's vibration to its optimal state. Since different frequencies in the crystals vibrate at frequencies that correspond with the different vibrational frequencies of your emotions, they can be used to restore stasis, counterbalance negative emotion or bring about a desired emotion. For instance, jade is believed to have a vibrational frequency that is the same as the one that your body reaches when you are in a state of relaxation. Therefore, using jade during times of stress may help to counterbalance the vibrations created by stressful emotions. Likewise, rose quartz, which vibrates at the same frequency as your body during states of emotional balance, can be used to restore balance during times of extreme emotionalism.

No matter what modality is used, the important concept to grasp here is that your energy can be changed and balanced. You don't have to be at the mercy of quantum entanglement and the moods and emotions of other people. Nor do you have to be at the mercy of your own thoughts that may have been programmed into your subconscious mind several decades ago. You have options and choices. It is up to you.

With quantum psychology and numerology, you have access to the information you need to understand the way your thoughts and emotions impact your body and your life, and how you can create positive changes.

Chapter 5

The Incredible Power of Beliefs

A great attitude does much more than turn on the lights in our worlds; it seems to magically connect us to all sorts of serendipitous opportunities that were somehow absent before the change.
~Earl Nightingale

When you take a moment to think about it, do you sometimes feel that your life is creating you instead of you creating your life? Do you feel in control of your thoughts and experiences or at the mercy of them? Well, that no longer has to be the case for you. You can now choose to control your emotional reactions to challenges and obstacles and control and form your thoughts so that they become useful to your visions and goals.

According to quantum psychology, your thoughts and perceptions have a huge affect on your experience of the world. Negative thought patterns can and do affect everything in your life—from your health and wellness to your prosperity and happiness.

The Power of Your Beliefs

It's no secret that some people are more successful than others. But the question is...*why*? Many people have the concept that truly amazing and/or successful individuals were "handed all the right cards in life," such as a powerful family, wealth or great parents and a childhood with a stable, balanced home life. How true is this assumption? Or...are successful people smarter, better at business in general, or do they have 'something' that other people lack?

If we look back in history, we will see that it's not necessarily any of the above. Rather, it's something in the internal operating system of their brains. Look at Mahatma Gandhi, Ho Chi Min or the Wright Brothers. None of these people came from powerful backgrounds or great wealth. They were common individuals, yet they accomplished great things because they expected nothing less of themselves.

The operating system within the brain is the place where individuals determine what they expect from themselves. And people always live up (or down) to their own expectations. If you expect to fail...you will. If you expect to be the CEO of a company...you will! It's all in the power of your beliefs.

The human belief is a very powerful thing. Many people don't realize that they actually set themselves up for failure without ever saying a word. Your internal feelings and beliefs about yourself are so powerful that they can either 'make you or break you.'

The reality is that life always has its ups and downs—even for those with powerful belief systems—but your belief system is what determines how you respond to the experiences of life and whether or not you believe that negatives can be turned into positives and that you can learn from your mistakes. In other words, taking less successful ideas and turning them into feedback and tools for learning rather than looking at them as 'failures.' The formula for success lies in correcting and tweaking 'the system.'

Your beliefs not only affect your thinking, they also affect your health and well being. A great illustration of this is the "Placebo Effect." In one study, patients were randomly selected to receive either a "sugar pill" or an analgesic for a headache, without the patient knowing that some of them were being given the sugar pills. Needless to say, the researchers were quite surprised when the people taking the sugar pill—because they believed they had received an analgesic—had close to the same results as those who had actually received the pain medication.

What this tells us is that what people perceive and believe is what they experience. The individuals who received the sugar pill believed that the medication would work for their headache, so it did. The placebo effect is so strong that even the FDA acknowledges the fact that individuals can benefit from a "fake" pill simply because they believe in it.

In another study, one group of participants was given a stimulant and the other a depressant but each group was told they were given the opposite. The results of each individual were actually more in line with the medication that they thought they had been given than the one they actually had received. Those receiving the stimulant felt drowsy and groggy because they believed they had received a depressant and those who were given the depressant felt full of energy. Their experience was the exact opposite of the actual effects of the medication because they told themselves how they believed they were supposed to be feeling and that's what they felt! The placebo effect is so strong that even the FDA acknowledges the fact that individuals can benefit from a "fake" pill because they believe in it.

In another example, a young teacher was told that she would be teaching a group of gifted students. In reality, the students fell in the average range of intelligence and had behavior problems as well. The teacher soon discovered that the students were not engaged, interested or able to behave with her current teaching style. However, because she believed that they were all gifted, she worked hard to come up with a teaching style that sparked the students' curiosity. In one year's time, this teacher increased the students' IQ with a jump of 20-30 points. The reason? She believed they were gifted and adjusted her behaviors to accommodate her beliefs.

That's how powerful your belief system is! And this power can be used to your advantage when creating a happy and successful life. Remember, what you believe is what you will create!

We all have a set of beliefs about a variety of things we experience every day, yet our beliefs are not set in stone, nor are they rules that we have to live by. Beliefs are mostly opinions or personal perceptions of a situation and sometimes perceptions are wrong, off, or misguided because of faulty information. And your beliefs (which affect your thoughts), can be changed.

Remember the game that most of us played in elementary school called "telephone?" It began with one person whispering a secret in the ear of the person standing next to them and this continued down a long line of students. By the end of the line, the details of the initial "secret" had changed, stories were different and perceptions were definitely different...the original statement had become distorted. Beliefs and perceptions can be affected the same way. Therefore, examine your beliefs to determine whether they are actually true or if they are tainted because of a past experience or another motive that may inhibit your ability.

The best way to examine whether your belief is a positive influence in your life or a negative one is to ask yourself whether that particular belief holds you back or empowers you. Most successful individuals share the belief that all things happen for a reason and that their lives are not ruled by "fate." Having a belief that only "fate" or "luck" or "a blessing" provides a successful outcome can cause distress and frustration. The reality is that success does not fall in anyone's lap, you have to make it happen and a healthy, empowering belief system can help you do just that. Change your thoughts about your beliefs and you can change your life.

True, success doesn't happen over night; it often takes time and patience and tapping into your creative resources can sometimes be an experience of trial and error. But as you grow in your success, you also learn about your own strengths and limitations. Throughout our lifetimes, we all have situations that we can look at and see great opportunities or we can look at and see as something that will not work or is a waste of our time. Opportunity isn't about 'luck,' it is about how you look at it and code it inside of your brain. Believing in yourself is the absolute most important step of any venture you embark on. By taking on new challenges and telling yourself that you will succeed, you can prove yourself right!

Examining Your Beliefs

Now that we've established the power of beliefs, it's important to understand that a belief that you hold can be untrue or a misconception, yet that does not minimize its power. We are all a product of our internal belief system, no matter how faulty that belief system may be. If you believe that you are a loser, your mind will help you make choices to support that belief even though in reality, you are not a loser!

People become what they believe because that is how they perceive the opportunity and environment around them. People do not perceive reality, but merely their perception (or belief) of reality. For instance, when two people have a verbal argument, they will both recall things differently. Each person's mind will take in parts of the altercation, changing, deleting and even distorting the information to match their own perception.

Because of the strength of our belief systems, people have self-fulfilling prophecies, not by accident but because they set themselves up for the situation. For example, a nagging, suspicious wife can drive her husband away with constant negativity. Our strong, passionate beliefs oftentimes come true because we continue with behaviors that support them until they are a reality.

Even though you may currently have a negative belief system, it doesn't have to stay that way, it can change. If you have a belief that is holding you back, you can change that belief to one that will help you succeed. Most successful individuals share a common belief that all things happen for a reason and not because of fate. The belief that fate or blessings provide a successful outcome can cause distress or frustration. Success does not fall into anyone's lap, they have to make it happen! And what each of us believes is possible is what we will create.

Prior to the 1950's no one had ever run a mile in less than four minutes. However, not long after Roger Bannister, a college student, ran a mile in less than four minutes, thirty-seven other runners broke the same record that year. Why had these same people not run at that speed before? The answer is simple: people fail to reach for what they think is unobtainable.

In fact, sometimes the brain will actually delete something because of a belief system. For instance, have you ever been looking for something and even though you searched everywhere you couldn't find it? All the while you were looking for it, you were probably telling yourself that you would not be able to find it...so you didn't. Yet someone else came along and easily found it in a space where you had already looked, at least two or three times! Why? Were you having trouble with your sight? No, this phenomenon is known as a "perceptual blind spot." Because you were busy telling yourself that you wouldn't find the object, your eyes scanned right across the item without detecting it. This is a negative visual hallucination. This idea of "blind spots" can extend to areas of success, health, wealth and all other facets of our experience. For instance, if you believe that there are no opportunities and that you will never be successful, you will miss them...even opportunities that may be right in front of you!

Real or Imagined?

We all have built-in 'tools' that we can use to change our belief systems and perceptions and our imagination is one of the most powerful! Medical science has proven that our brain does not differentiate what is vividly imagined from what has been actually experienced. The same neurological impulses are triggered throughout the nervous system for both situations. This is a powerful fact that can be used to help 'prepare yourself for success'. By using visualizations or closing your eyes and imagining yourself achieving what you desire to accomplish, you are "programming" your brain to help you do just that.

Let's test out the theory:

Think of a large yellow lemon...the mere name signifies sour. Now close your eyes and imagine biting into that lemon. The sour juice drenches your tongue, making your nose twitch and your mouth pucker. Feel the cold surface of the lemon on your hands and close to your nose. Smell the citrus scent, reminding you of how sour it really tastes.

Are you salivating? The answer is probably a resounding "Yes!" because your nervous system has been activated just as if you had that lemon in your mouth.

This power of imagination can work to your benefit or it can work against you. Some people begin to feel fear or stress at the mere sound of a certain situation which can actually create health problems because when the fear response is activated, the immune system can be suppressed, making the person more prone to illness. Or you can use the power of your imagination to your benefit.

For years, the Russians have dominated the Olympic Games in gymnastics and many have wondered why the performances of the Russian athletes are always so excellent. What's the secret? They understand the power of the mind and belief system! The Russian Olympic team employs a sports psychologist who teaches them psychological techniques that enhance the athletes' physical techniques. They are not only preparing their bodies for victory, but their minds as well.

Think about it for a minute...when you rehearse failure in your mind, what are you likely to do? On the other hand, if you follow the example of the Russian gymnasts and their secret mental preparedness, you can succeed just as they do. When you rehearse the pictures of success in your mind, you soon will be experiencing them in person.

Using Visualizations

Visualizing is a very important aspect of human behavior. With the power of visualization, you can see yourself accomplishing anything you want to accomplish. You can picture any and all aspects of your life exactly as you want them to be. You can imagine breaking through the limitations and boundaries that are holding you back.

Everyone of us has the power to visualize, which is the act of concentrating and projecting what we want onto our minds. But there is a lot more that goes on. When we visualize, we are actually causing a high frequency of energy to propagate in the universe. In other words, we are changing the speed at which we vibrate and it is the speed of the vibration that changes the form that energy takes. And changes in frequency alone bring about vastly different results. When we change our vibrations through visualization, the law of attraction ensures that the 'signal' is captured and the image in our mind will be transmitted back to us. Visualization can help us step beyond boundaries that we are currently imposing on ourselves.

Try this exercise to help you see the power of visualization:

- Pointing your finger forward, and without moving your feet, turn your body in a clockwise motion as far as you can. Make a mental note of this position.
- Close your eyes and visualize yourself in the above exercise.
- Now, with your eyes closed, continue, but stretch yourself a little further (in your mind). Imagine yourself turning three feet further than you turned the first time.
- Now open your eyes and repeat the first exercise. You went further than the first time, right?

The point is that you can get past the mental limits and boundaries you set for yourself. That's because when you imagine you can, you do! Success is just a visualization away. Yet most people may strive to reach a record, but never seek to break that record, never going after higher goals for themselves.

Create Your Beliefs

The lesson in all of this is to carefully examine your beliefs and decide whether or not you want to live the reality of your current belief system because you could create a self-fulfilling prophecy that you don't want. On the other hand, if you create a positive, supportive belief system, you can create a life and future you really do want! Never take the "top goal" and quit. Strive for more and reach for the unthinkable! hen you find a belief that is not working to your best and highest good, change your thinking around it.

Our beliefs come from our experiences as well as the people around us. We draw them from our friends, family members, educators, famous people and local heroes. Our perceptions and beliefs make us who we are, but they are never absolute truths and should be treated as such. It is important that you constantly evaluate your beliefs to ensure that they are not holding you back. Remember, beliefs become embedded in our brains and become our behaviors which create our lives!

To Change Your Life, Change Your Thinking

Changing your life starts with changing your thinking. And the first step to changing your thinking is to identify the thought patterns (or beliefs) that don't serve you and replacing them with thought patterns that do. This may sound simple and impossible all at the same time. With some awareness of your negative thought patterns, you can consciously begin to change your thoughts to those that will lead to positive outcomes in your life.

For many, finding that new way of thinking is triggered by an epiphany or what Oprah Winfrey refers to as an "Ah Ha! Moment." While it seems that such moments are spontaneous, it is more often true than new thought patterns are arrived at through careful and deliberate inner work.

Although there are factors (as the study of numerology points out) that help determine what areas of our life may be like, it is still our beliefs, our thought processes and our decisions that have the final say. This story about a Zen Master and his disciple clearly explains the association between what is "a given" and what is "a matter of choice."

Many years ago there was a Zen Master who never failed to come up with an answer to every question that his disciples asked him. But one of his disciples was determined to challenge the master and find a question that had no answer. So one day on the way to school, this disciple saw a wounded bird fall from its nest and suddenly he knew he had the perfect unanswerable question. He picked up the bird and gently carried it to the school. When he saw the Zen master, he cried out, "Dear Master, can you tell me whether the bird in my hand is alive or dead?" Smiling, he confidently waited for the master to respond as he was sure that there would be no answer. To the student's surprise, the Master smiled and replied, "My dear student, if I say the bird in alive, you will tighten your grip and it will die, and I will be wrong. However, if I say the bird is dead, you will release your grip and let go of the bird. Again, my answer will be wrong. Thus, the right answer lies in your hand, and that I cannot answer."

The moral of this story is that the answer lies in our choices. It is up to us to decide what is best. We each become what we choose no matter what the circumstances may be.

Cherish your visions and your dreams as they are the children of your soul, the blueprints of your ultimate achievements.
~Napoleon Hill

Chapter 6

The Power of Intention

*Our minds are finite, and yet even in these circumstances of
finitude we are surrounded by possibilities that are infinite, and
the purpose of life is to grasp
as much as we can out of that infinitude.*
~Alfred North Whitehead

Intention and Success

Success in life can be described as a continuous journey in
which we seek happiness, explore spirituality and work
diligently and progressively towards the realization of our
goals. Contrary to popular belief, capability is not based on
intelligence but is strongly impacted by attitude. Those who
look at new challenges or change with a positive spirit can
acquire new skills and capabilities. It is the power of your
intention that can strongly affect everything you do.

As previously discussed, thought has both a physical basis
and an energetic one. Once you think a thought, it is always
tied to you, but it also exists out in the quantum soup that
makes up our universe. We already know that this quantum
soup is made up of particles and waves existing in a state of
pure possibility surrounded by vast empty spaces. All of this
exists just waiting for the observer to appear to collapse the
possibility into perceptual reality.

It is into this quantum soup that your thought appears like a magnet to draw whatever it contains to it. Remember, everything exists only in a state of pure possibility until there is interaction with an observer. In this case, you are the observer and your thought is what is affecting the wave function collapse from a state of pure possibility to a state of perceptual reality. Your thought draws to you the outcome contained inside of that thought.

As previously explained, under the right set of circumstances, thoughts can become things. But what are the right set of circumstances for this to happen? Focus, attention and intention can all combine to make what you think about manifest in your life.

It is an ability that we all posses, though most of us are unaware of the magic that lies inside of our minds. The human mind is a learning machine! Merely by thinking, each and every human on this planet can turn the possibility that exists in the quantum soup into the perceived reality that exists within our physical universe. Therein lies the power and potential as an amazing tool for creating the life you want: through the power of thought and intention, you can draw to your life exactly what you choose.

It sounds easy, but the truth is that it requires focused intention. The reason that we very seldom experience the manifestation of our thoughts into realities is because our brains are all over the place. In one moment we can visualize the most amazing outcomes, and in the next we are overcome by doubt, frustration and negativity. Having focused intention to manifest reality requires an effort to control your thoughts and visualizations so that they are all pointing towards the same outcome. It requires significant conscious effort to be aware of your counter-productive thoughts and to re-channel them so they attract only those things you desire.

There are a number of exercises you can do to help you stay focused in intention.

- Visualization is one.
- Affirmations are another…speaking a series of "I am" and "I have" statements on a regular basis can help you to focus and strengthen your intention.
- Acting as if you already have that which you are drawing towards you is another technique that works well.

In Your Business Life

Can the knowledge of quantum psychology affect how business is done in today's world? It may surprise you to know that the answer is a resounding "yes!" By consciously monitoring and channeling your thoughts around your business, you can attract exactly what you choose.

On your own, this might be a task you feel capable of doing, but in a business filled with people, this task becomes challenging because it requires not only a common vision, but also a collective effort to achieve laser-like focused intention. Yet it can be done.

As a business professional or business owner, you can harness principles of quantum psychology to help your business. Begin with yourself:

- First, create your vision. What is it that you want your business to achieve?
- Next, set your intention. For example, say that you want your business to attract a certain type of client. Who is that client? What do they look like? How do they act? What are their goals? How will they come to you?
- Get a picture of your "ideal client" in your head. See them and experience them in your mind, and put yourself in the picture, interacting with them and meeting their business needs.
- Visualize exactly what you want to attract to your business with yourself in the picture.

Then include your team in the process because if the intention of one person is powerful, then the intention of multiple people all focused in the same direction is even more so. Once you have a clear and focused picture of your vision, it is time to communicate that vision to your team. Share your vision and intention with them and inspire them to participate fully in that vision by setting their intention as well. As a business leader, it is up to you to have such clear vision and intention that you inspire those on your team to share your vision and make your intention theirs.

The exercises of visualization, affirmations and 'acting as if' that have been previously mentioned can also work for your business and can be done alone or as a team to help everyone involved in your business stay focused in intention. For instance, preparing your presentation or proposal for the client you have visualized can be a powerful tool in drawing that client closer to you.

Focus, attention and intention can all combine to make what you think about manifest in your business. And the more people who are directing their focus, intention and attention towards a common goal, the more quickly what is being focused on will become manifest. It's like a magnet. The bigger the magnet, the stronger the pull. So it is with large amounts of energy from focused intention. When groups of people all focus their intention together, then the magnetic pull is exponentially larger than when a single person focuses alone.

This is why having a team with a common goal and a shared intention can mean the difference between success and failure. As a matter of fact, a shared vision amongst team members is more important than the talent level of each of the members because the focused visualizations of the team becomes a magnet that goes out into the quantum ooze and attracts the solid manifestation of the shared vision.

On the surface, it would seem that shared vision drives success because all of the team members are working towards the same goal and are therefore willing to work harder. While that is part of the reason, it isn't the entire reason that common vision is so important.

If you have a team full of talented players, then that is certainly part of the formula; however, when everyone focuses on a shared vision, it is then that apparent business miracles will happen. In reality, it isn't miraculous at all. It is merely the logical outcome of the application and understanding of the laws that underlie our universe.

A quantum business model is no place for wimps. There is no room for doubts. Keep your thoughts intentionally focused, and you will attract to your business exactly what you visualize for it.

The Power of Intention

No matter where in your life you focus your intention, you will create change. Since thoughts become reality, intentionally focusing your thoughts on certain behaviors or possibilities will bring them into reality. Once you ensure that your belief system is in alignment with what you desire in life, concentrating on and paying attention to those beliefs will focus your attention on them and the power of your intention will bring them into reality.

Chapter 7

Neuro-Linguistic Programming (NLP) And Hypnosis

This world conceals everything,
unless you're ready to undo it.
Then, everything appears as a piece of the infinite
and you are no different from it.
~Brita LaTona

<u>Changing Your Life</u>

While it often feels as if we have very little control over our thoughts and emotions, there are ways by which we can program ourselves to replace negative thoughts with positive ones. By shifting your thinking patterns or patterns of behavior, you can change your life and even define a new direction instead of continuing to do the same things that have not produced the effects that you desire.

Hypnosis and NLP are different than traditional talk therapy and can help you to begin choosing positive thoughts by overriding the subconscious. When the principles of quantum psychology and numerology are combined with therapy techniques such as hypnosis and neuro-linguistic programming (NLP), it is possible to reprogram your old thought patterns and habits, change weaknesses or enhance strengths to influence and change your life.

NLP uses a series of simple physical anchors that are keyed to positive thoughts and emotions. The anchors can be deployed whenever you notice yourself slipping into negativity, causing a change in your thought patterns.

Hypnosis uses a similar mechanism, but uses post-hypnotic suggestion when your consciousness is at its most suggestible in order to override negative thought patterns of which you may be completely unaware.

Both NLP and hypnosis are techniques which can help to alter the structure of your thinking and perceptions by providing you with a mechanism by which you can shift from negative subconscious thought patterns to positive ones.

Hypnosis

In hypnosis, the change is done through suggestion when your mind is in a deeply relaxed and suggestive state. Oftentimes people are concerned that with hypnosis they give up control of their mind. In actuality, you will be able to hear and remember everything that occurs during your hypnosis. The process of hypnosis simply bypasses the conscious mind in order to get to the source of any fears or negative thought patterns that have been built up through a lifetime of conditioning and programming.

When you are in a deeply relaxed state, your subconscious mind is more willing and able to receive and internalize helpful suggestions because the conscious mind is not involved. A skilled hypnotherapist can help you discover the source of much of your world-view as well as work with you in making changes to those thought patterns and beliefs that are destructive to your current goals. Hypnosis allows you to bypass your conscious point of view to reformulate how you see the universe. Once a hypnotic state is achieved, your mind is open and suggestible to change. Simple post-hypnotic suggestions made in a trance state can help you build a defense against negativity, or, conversely, be more open to intuition and positive messages.

Neuro-Linguistic Programming (NLP)

NLP differs from hypnosis in that there is no need for a trance state. And, NLP can be used on its own or in conjunction with hypnotherapy. By using simple gestures or triggers, NLP can replace harmful thoughts and beliefs with ones that are more helpful and productive. It is based on the theory that by remodeling your negative thoughts, you can change your life. This technique allows you to bypass filters (either your own or others) to establish rapport and then anchor certain thoughts, beliefs, emotions and behaviors that can then be triggered through simple physical actions.

Most therapy is remedial in that it is directed toward solving problems of the past. NLP, however, teaches skills that promote positive changes, which in turn generate new possibilities and opportunities. NLP can help you become adept at whatever you want to do.

For instance, NLP can:

- Change a past impact on a business client.
- Turn a poor speller to an excellent speller.
- Assist a person in gaining rapport nonverbally.

- Help an athlete improve concentration.
- Be used as a method of therapy.
- Serve as a process of teaching people to use their minds.
- Help a person become a better communicator in their relationships.

By combining the knowledge of the way that the brain works along with observations of how a person relates to his or her life (both consciously and subconsciously) and any limiting beliefs that may exist, NLP can be used to help people understand the power they have over their thoughts and beliefs. Thus they have power over their life and changing their life.

Using Symbols in Neuro-Linguistic Programming (NLP)

As we discussed in Chapter 3, we are constantly affected by symbols and the subconscious meaning and perceptions to which those meanings are attached to our lives. The good news is that symbols can be consciously used to reprogram those areas of your mind and your life that you want to change and improve.

NLP is a psychological modality that allows you to reset your programming and create the models of the world that you generate. Instead of being at the mercy of all of the psychological presets and filters that you have in place, NLP can help you respond to symbols in ways that positively affect your behaviors.

Symbols such as gestures, sounds or images can be used to anchor the feelings, thoughts and beliefs that you want to have or that are productive to where you want to go in life.

For example, suppose you long to experience a sense of peace. Close your eyes and visualize the most peaceful place that you can remember. Maybe it was in the mountains, on a beach or in the presence of someone you love. Make your visualization as vivid as you possibly can and explore it with your five senses. Allow yourself to feel how emotionally peaceful you are in that situation. Now touch your right hand to your right cheek while you are still in that visualization and in that place. You have just set a symbolic anchor (in this case the gesture of touching your right hand to your right cheek) that can help you to move into a place of peace merely be repeating the symbolic gesture. It may take a few visualizations and a few times of repeating the process, but eventually when you touch your right hand to your right cheek, you will find yourself emotionally in that place of peace.

This is the power of NLP. By selecting programmed responses to symbols that we experience—whether they are verbal, visual, audible or even gestures—we choose our responses rather than reacting to everyday symbols in a manner that is unconscious. Using NLP and the power of symbols, you can transform your life.

Using the Information From Numerology as a Guide

In numerology, people can discover certain traits or characteristics that might be inherent and are affecting their thought processes and belief systems. Once discovered on a conscious basis, NLP can be used to impact and change those subconscious belief systems.

For instance, according to numerology, two of the weaknesses for the character number 4 are: they are insecure and impatient. Using this information, NLP can help in retraining or reprogramming their responses to improve their sense of self and their patience.

For Business Applications

NLP provides a simple tool that you can use to help focus your team so that you all share a common vision. By learning the basics of this method, you can anchor certain behaviors and thought processes in your employees so that you can harness the power of group-focused intention. Knowledge of NLP techniques can also help to focus communication among your team members so that you can better relate to one another, which aids in the communication of a common vision.

Not only does NLP help with focusing your team so that you can attract to your business the types of customers and clients you desire, but it can also be used when you are working with those clients to find the best business solution to meet their needs. The same simple anchoring process can enhance communications with your customers and help them to become part of your overall vision of success and achievement.

Putting It All Together

By understanding the laws of the universe at its tiniest levels, accessing the knowledge available through numerology and having the conscious awareness that you have the ability to change your energy and thoughts which can change your life, you take the power of change into your own hands. You're at the helm. You get to choose. You do not have to be a ship that is at the mercy of the wind and waves, but can be one that is using the power in the wind and waves to navigate your chosen course.

Chapter 8

Using Your Values as a Driving Force

It doesn't matter who you are, where you come from. The ability to triumph begins with you. Always.
~Oprah Winfrey

Have you ever heard someone say that when people are driven by their emotions rather than logic, it is their downfall? It is true that people often take action based on the way they feel, because they are human. A creature who was 100 percent logical would act like a robot, lacking emotion along with empathy for others. Yet, the reality is that emotions and feelings are sometimes a restricting force for many. For instance, if someone is fearful or lacking motivation or self-confidence, these responses are emotional and not logical.

Emotions or feelings basically fall into two categories: negative or positive, and as human beings we instinctively move toward positive emotions and away from negative ones without logically looking at those choices. For instance, a person can logically know that smoking or over-eating can cause them great harm. Yet they will continue the habit because of the feelings such as a sense of control or a sense of calmness that doing the behavior provides. There is an emotional payout behind the behavior.

Positive Versus Negative Emotions

Do you remember watching amoebas in junior high science class? Under the magnifying glass you could see the tiny organisms as they moved toward food and away from a source of heat. They were responding to positive and negative forces in their environment. They moved toward food which was a positive experience for them and away from heat which created a negative experience. The same theory applies to people. As a whole, we moved toward success, freedom and happiness and away from rejection, embarrassment, sadness....

We all want to experience positive emotions, yet we do not all attach the same feelings to the same situations. For instance, people who have attached positive emotions to having a relationship and getting married will put a lot of effort into creating situations that can help them achieve this goal. On the other hand, people who view marriage or a relationship as a loss of freedom and an environment filled with discord will wish to avoid the experience.

The Impact of Values

Values are not the same for everyone. What is success for one may not matter to another even though the value may be the same. For instance, many people claim to value success, yet what is success for one person may not be success for someone else. The difference often lies in the emotional significance that a person holds in reference to success. One person may define success as making millions of dollars every year while another person may define success as being able to save a life. No two people are the same. We all individually define our own values.

For example, if a person is deeply drawn to security and consistency, he or she would be most likely to avoid risky behavior, be a spend thrift or have a flashy job that was not secure. This individual would live very differently from someone who attached positive emotions to excitement, change and spending money.

Even if people value something in the same way, they will often work very differently to achieve that goal. The reason for this is because of what is important to them or what positive emotions they have attached to what they value.

Let's look at Mother Teresa and Madonna who are two women who both longed to touch the lives of people and have great success in doing so. They both put great value on being able to succeed in that goal. And they both succeeded in touching millions of lives. However, while their goals were similar, the way they achieved those goals was extremely different. While Madonna touched lives through music and songs that lifted the spirits of millions, Mother Teresa touched millions by feeding the hungry and bringing comfort through spirituality. While the value of success was the same for both of them, the roads they took to achieve that goal were far from the same.

Analyzing Your Values

To truly understand how you have become who you are, it is important to understand the values that you are moving toward as well as what you are moving away from. These 'away from' values are just as important to understand as your 'toward' values. That comprehension can provide you with guidance in recognizing any issues or problems that may be holding you back from your own definition of success.

Understanding that significant emotions drive values can often help explain the success or lack thereof in your life. After discovering your own values and what you are moving toward or away from can give you a good indication of where you are going in your life.

Since it is very hard to change what you do not know or what you have not acknowledged, once you determine your 'toward' and 'away from' values, you will be able to recognize some of the thoughts, beliefs and emotions that are creating problems for you and impeding your ability to accomplish your goals and desires.

Changing Your Values

Sometimes the emotion that we have attached to a value is detrimental to us. For instance, we may have unconsciously attached an emotion of fear around having a lot of money because we have a belief that people with a lot of money can be targets of crime. This negative value or emotion that is attached to having a lot of money may actually be moving us away from something that we believe we are trying hard to achieve.

But values can be changed, and NLP is one of the modalities that can be used for this change. Once a new value is determined, it is important to take steps toward achieving the goal. These steps include making a plan, mapping it out and then following through. This may mean making new choices, changing habits or living a little differently. Through rehearsal and envisioning yourself in that success light, you will find the positive image you need for moving forward.

Chapter 9

Working Within the Logical Levels of Change

*They must often change, who would be constant in
happiness or wisdom.*
~Confucius

Taking the power of change into your own hands is like getting behind the wheel of your vehicle—you are then in the driver's seat. You get to choose the path of your journey, the speed at which you will travel and your final destination. Yet there is one important step you must take first, and that is to decide that you want to go somewhere in the first place. Or in the case of change, you must acknowledge that there is a need for some reshaping in your life and that you definitely want to guide the force and direction of those alterations.

Once you've said 'yes' to change, it is important to create a foundation for that transformation and to understand the reason behind the change. First of all, get clear on what level of your life needs changing. Is it on a personal level, a business level, an emotional level or a combination of several different areas of your life?

The Purpose Behind Your Desired Change

There is always a motivating reason behind change. This purpose is often larger than a person's identity, yet there are times that people will journey through life questioning their purpose when it is often right in front of them. They are simply looking too hard. Purpose and passion are most often tied together. If you have passion about something, look closely and you will often be able to clearly see your purpose as well.

Passion and purpose are often the fuel for the engine of change because having a passion for something will generally keep a person on track for much longer than when passion is not present. There have been countless cases when individuals have continued to persevere through hard times and even suffering because their passion for their purpose was greater than any other motivating force in their life. The Dalai Lama, Martin Luther King, and Mother Teresa are all very good examples of this.

If the change you want to make in your life is motivated by a passion or a purpose, these two guiding forces can help you stay on track and headed for your goal regardless of any conflict or troubles that may cross your path. Do you have a purpose for your life? Are you motivated by a passion for something? Answering the following questions can help you find out:

- What is the reason you are here on this Earth?
- What can you contribute to this earth or to those around you during your lifetime?
- How do you want to be remembered when you die?
- What strengths can you use to contribute to a higher good?

First Things First

The best way to understand whether or not the revamping you want to do is a good choice and to determine your best plan of action is to ask yourself some very important questions...who-what-where-why and how.

Who – From your core level...who are you in regard to your capabilities, your beliefs, your values, your sense of self? Understanding who you are from this level will help you make the decisions that will need to be made in order to facilitate change.

What - What actions are you willing to take to move yourself toward change? What behaviors are you willing to modify? What part of your belief system are you willing to examine and perhaps revamp?

Where – This has to do with the environment in which you currently exist. Your current environment can sometimes be the problem or the constraint that is holding you back from change. Sometimes your environment can be altered and at other times you have to find a way around it.

Why – This is the reason for your change. Your beliefs and values are often the motivational base that allows you to begin the transformation itself. If you know why you want to revamp your thoughts, actions or life, you have a powerful beginning to help drive you through the journey of the adjustment.

How – These are the steps that you will need to take in order to go from where you are now to where you want to be. The 'how' in the equation of change is about what you know, what you are capable of doing and the transformation that can be accomplished with that skill set.

Making Small Steps

Once your foundation and plan of action have been determined, it's time to take some small steps to start moving you in that direction. Oftentimes when people decide they want to change, they'll take one big giant step and want the transformation to happen all at one time. This approach can cause them to be overwhelmed by the whole process which can throw them back to the beginning, feeling frustrated and discouraged. It's much better to take a series of small steps that will eventually bring you to where you want to be.

Think of creating change in your life as being similar to updating your home. Once you know how you want your home to look when you are done, it's much easier to start by thinking of colors, decorations and minor repairs which will enable you to begin the process and get a sense of accomplishment before you tackle the higher levels of change such as electrical, plumbing or replacing the carpeting and flooring. If you start with smaller projects and the process of mapping out a system of steps that can help you get prepared for the larger ones, you will then be ready for the financial or emotional price that those larger projects can require.

The same goes for when you are making changes on the internal and external parts of who you are. As you take smaller, manageable steps toward your desired change, you will build confidence that will help you to better handle the deeper levels of transformation that may be required in accomplishing your overall goal. Another way to think of the importance of taking steps in your process of change is to compare it to a person who wants to climb to the top of a high mountain. They cannot realistically expect to take one giant step in hopes of reaching the top. They understand that there will be a series of smaller steps that will help them condition themselves in their journey to the highest peak. The same is true in the journey toward achieving our goals.

An NLP Roadmap

When NLP is used as a tool for change, there is a 'roadmap' that is used to help guide the different levels of change and the order in which they should be addressed:

1. **Identity**
2. **Beliefs and Values**
3. **Capabilities and Skills**
4. **Behavior**
5. **Environment**

Using this methodology for change helps keep your thought patterns and perceptions in alignment with your overall goals. The reason that a process is important is because our brain is a vast informational system that has a series of maps that increase with the input of new information and experiences. Because of the extensive territory around these 'maps' in our brains, our current perceptions can sometimes limit the incoming information and actually prevent any adjustments we are trying to make. In fact, sometimes our perspective on new experiences, tasks or information can actually guide us in the wrong direction. For this reason, it is imperative that we learn to control our thinking and the order in which we provide ourselves with new information as we consciously choose to transform an area or areas of our life.

Let's look a little closer at each one of these areas and their significance when it comes to creating change.

Identity

Some people think that identity is based on skills, intelligence and behavior. NLP, however, looks at the definition of identity of a person separate from that of their behavior. Instead of lumping people into a category based on their actions, NLP sees behavior as a consequence of an underlying motive. This belief is an optimistic view of mankind which avoids attaching labels to people based on their behavior.

For instance, if you attach your behavior to your identity and you are not happy with a particular behavior, that means that you would not be happy with yourself as a whole which could cause you to develop the perception that your character as a whole was flawed. This would be untrue. We need to learn to separate our behavior from who we are in order to avoid a negative effect to the identity level of who we are as an individual.

If you have some confusion around who you are as an individual or surrounding your identity, asking yourself some questions can help you clear up this confusion.

- How do you feel about yourself?
- How do you express yourself?
- How do others feel about you?

- Do you label yourself according to your behaviors?
- Do you label others according to their behaviors?
- Do other people have an accurate picture of who you really are?
- If not, why not?

Beliefs and Values

As previously discussed, beliefs and values are what drive us to either achieve our goals or to get lost in trying. The way we feel about something, especially one of our goals or a change we want to make, either motivates us to continue on or discourages us from even trying. To begin with, working toward a goal is not always easy and success does not happen overnight. Because of these realities, motivation is imperative for helping us accomplish our desires. Our beliefs not only keep us moving toward the end result, they also help us rank our wants and our desires.

For example, if you have a choice of playing a round of golf or going to work, the decision might be a hard one to make until your belief and value systems step in. You might get great recognition for playing a good round of golf, but if you don't go to work, you won't get paid, or you could possibly lose your job. Your beliefs and value system around these consequences are what will help you easily make your choice.

Beliefs also keep us in the place or environment in which we need to be. For example, if our goal is to get into shape, that desire is most achievable by spending time in the gym or a fitness area and not at the ice cream parlor.

If you need some help in clarifying your beliefs and values when it comes to your goals or the changes you want to make, start by asking yourself questions such as:

- What is important to you and why?
- What are your beliefs around what is right and what is wrong?
- What are your beliefs around the changes you want to make or the goals you want to achieve?
- What are your values around these changes or goals?
- What do you believe is important to other people?

Capabilities and Skills

Because the human mind is a learning machine, there is no doubt that some people have inborn skills and/or talents. We all know people who seem more "capable" than others and oftentimes mistakenly think that these abilities are based on their intelligence. However, most researchers, business owners and people in general now understand that the best employees are those who are team oriented and have a positive attitude. People who have a positive attitude or spirit when it comes to change or challenges can acquire any new skills or capabilities that are needed for the process.

The core theory in NLP is based on the fact that all skills are learnable and with the desire and a positive attitude, you can learn anything from riding a bike to snow skiing to how to interact with difficult people, and everything in between. NLP applies the theory that everyone has the capability of learning.

The following questions can help you get an idea of your own capabilities and establish a better understanding of where you can make some improvements:

- What are you good at?
- What do others often comment and give you compliments about?
- What is a skill that you learned in the past?
- What were the events, happenings or situations that led to your learning this skill?
- Can you recognize a pattern in that process that you can use for learning other skills?

Behavior

From an NLP perspective, behavior is not only your observable actions, it is also the way you feel about your actions. The reason for this is that how you feel about your behavior is generally the driving force behind the actions themselves, often inspiring them again and again. In fact, your feelings may well be the purpose that drives your behavior and until you understand that, you may have a difficult time making changes.

To achieve your goals and make your desired changes, it is very important that you maximize positive behavior. At first it will take a conscious effort to maximize the right behaviors until those actions become a part of your life and who you are—from choosing a salad at lunch or dinner or setting aside time for practicing to support your new- found love for golf.

In contrast, if there are behaviors that you no longer want as a part of your life, it will at first take conscious effort to decrease and then eliminate those actions. As you apply conscious effort to those choices, they will eventually disappear from your perspective of viable options.

Sometimes it is difficult to determine whether or not your behavior is in line with your goals. Taking time to ask yourself some questions on that perspective will help you ensure that it is and if not, will help you to know what new actions need to be integrated into your life.

- Do your behaviors help create happiness in your life?
- Are your actions consistent with your goals and desires?
- Is there a pattern to your behavior?
- If so, is that pattern consistent with your goals?
- Do you notice behavior patterns in others?
- What does your body language tell you about your behaviors and actions?
- Does your body language change in different situations?
- Is your body language giving you messages that are inconsistent with your goals and desires?

Environment

Your environment and surroundings are important aspects of your ability to make changes in your life. Your surroundings can sometimes be very supportive of change, but at other times they can be a hindrance in achieving any transformation. In fact, there are times that your environment might simply not be conducive to the changes you want to make. When that is the case, change could be difficult, if not impossible.

The good news is that you can realign your environment to a degree that can make it easier to achieve your goal. At times it can be as simple as surrounding yourself with people whose lives contain the behaviors that you wish to adopt. For example, if you want to learn a new language, it is much easier to do when you surround yourself with others who speak that new language. Or, if you want to make a change to becoming more optimistic and having a positive attitude, gravitate toward business associates and friends who exhibit those behaviors.

The following are some of the questions that you can ask yourself to help you determine whether or not your current environment supports your goals and desires:

- Where are you when you feel the happiest?
- What type of work environment helps you excel?
- Describe your ideal home environment.
- What time of day are you most productive?
- How closely do your answers align with the reality of your current environment?

Moving Forward

Now that you understand your motivation and the levels of change that exist in all of us and the order in which they should be addressed for ensuring your success, it's time to move forward. The practical steps listed below can help you move in the direction that you want to go.

Gather Your Information

No matter what change you have decided to make, whether it is eating healthier, improving your career, changing your personal life, etc., it is important that you get all of the facts that you need in order to make the right choices. Remember the process for writing a research paper? First you gathered all of the information and then you organized the information into a system that made creating the paper easy and logical.

The same goes for life. If you want to eat healthier, you need to first find out exactly what that means for you and then set up a system whereby you have the right food choices available for you when mealtimes come around or when you get hungry. Without having the right information or system available to help implement your change, you will most likely go right back to the choices you have been making in that area of your life.

Build Relationships

Relationships are a crucial part of life, both personal and business and creating supportive relationships can help in the process of change. For instance, building relationships with your family is important in a change because any transformation of one person typically changes the dynamics of the entire family. But building relationships in other areas of your life are important as well because of the support system it can create for you as you make the desired adjustments to your life.

Improve Performance

Once you have decided what area of your life needs changing and at what level that change needs to occur, it can be helpful to create a system whereby you can document your improvement. For instance, people who are trying to lose weight will often weigh themselves once a week to ensure that they are headed toward their goal. If the desire is to reduce your spending, creating a budget that documents your income and expenses from week to week will help you monitor your performance and build your sense of achievement along the way.

Build Self-Confidence

Change can be difficult and challenging, but as you take steps toward your desired change, take time to acknowledge your accomplishments and to feel good about what you are doing. We all need encouragement and sometimes those crucial words of praise need to come from ourselves.

Identifying the Logical Levels of Any Road Blocks

Any attempt toward change doesn't easily flow on a path with no bumps, detours or road blocks. They happen. But if we listen closely, whether it is to ourselves or to someone else who is trying to create change in their lives, it is often easy to determine which one of the logical levels of change is causing the problems simply by how they (or we) say something as much as what they (or we) say. Using the sentence below, pay attention to the word that is bolded and italicized and what statement that word is making.

I can't do it here.	Statement about identity.
I *can't* do it here.	Statement about beliefs.
I can't *do* it here.	Statement about capability.
I can't do *it* here.	Statement about behavior.
I can't do it *here.*	Statement about environment.

Understanding and Using the Logical Levels of Change

There are certain requirements that are needed for change: the desire to change, knowing how to change and creating the opportunity for change. Working within the logical levels of change can help you in deciding that you can make it happen, and accepting the fact that you have choices will assist you in the transformation process, helping to ensure your success.

Chapter 10

Connecting With Others

Our attitude toward others determines their attitude towards us.
~Earl Nightingale

Our success and happiness in life depend largely on our ability to interact and effectively connect with others. As is true for most things, there is a part of our brain, that when we understand and use it, can help us build rapport with other people. Connecting with or building rapport has a lot to do with our acceptance of each other, and research tells us that there are actually two areas of our brain that are involved in accepting people.

The first aspect has to do with memory or our recall of the way they look. The second level of acceptance is emotional and begins in a small part of our brain called the amygdala whose job it is to make an emotionally based threat assessment of every situation or person in our lives. A good portion of this assessment is based on how similar or dissimilar the person is to us. If we appear to be the same, our defenses stay relaxed and our acceptance is strong, but if we appear to be different, our defenses will rise and our acceptance minimizes.

Understanding Rapport

As we discussed in an earlier chapter, it is important to bypass our own filters as well as the filters of others to establish rapport with someone. Since rapport begins with acceptance and acceptance has a lot to do with whether or not we perceive someone to be like us or different from us, the first step in building rapport with someone is to meet them on their terms, not yours. This is just one of the steps you can take to help bypass predetermined perceptions. By doing so, you can also establish trust and credibility which will lead to rapport and relationships. Remember, people like others who are similar to them and understanding this one strong point can help you consciously connect with others.

Similarity does not necessarily have anything to do with how you look but can often be assumed by behaviors such as standing or sitting in the same positions, assuming the same postures or even talking about a topic on which you both agree. Often these similarities will take place between two people without them even being aware of it happening. For instance:

- Have you ever yawned just because someone else has yawned? It's not a conscious behavior, it is often an automatic response.
- Have you ever looked up when you noticed someone else looking up?
- Have you ever picked up an accent simply because you were speaking with someone who had an accent?

These behaviors are just some of the unconscious ways that people will become 'similar' to each other when they spend time together or are building rapport. Often, when you see a group of friends sitting together and conversing, if you look closely, you will notice that they are most likely sitting in the same position as well as making the same or similar hand and arm movements and gestures. This physical "mirroring" is just one of the ways that people subliminally connect.

Because most communication between people actually occurs on a non-verbal level, people are always generating information and communicating whether they are aware of it or not. Therefore, being mindful of the postures or behaviors that can lead to rapport can help you purposefully connect with people that you want to get to know.

Using Mirroring for Building Rapport

When people are together and they use the same gestures or sit in the same or similar positions, they are unconsciously "mirroring" each other in an effort to establish a connection. The examples we gave above of yawning, looking up and picking up an accent are all examples of "mirroring." When people have established a connection or rapport with each other, these actions will just naturally happen.

These techniques, however, can be purposefully applied to help you connect with one, several or many people. To apply the mirroring technique when you first meet someone, there are steps that you can take:

- Make eye contact.
- Physically match your posture to that of the other person.

- Change your breathing to breathe at the same rate as they are breathing.
- If they lean slightly, lean the same way.
- If they cross their legs, cross your legs,
- If they adjust their clothing, do the same.

Even though it may sound as though you are mimicking the other person, mirroring can be done in a way that eliminates the appearance of doing so. To begin with, don't move at the same pace as the other person but slow your responses down by a second or two to give you ample time to make your movements without seeming to mimic. It is also not necessary to move to the full extent that the other person has moved. Your motions should be fluid, relaxed and seemingly natural. Your intention is to create the feeling of similarity which will open the opportunity for building a connection.

There are several components to mirroring that can be practiced to help you in the area of building rapport.

Breathing

Mirroring someone's breathing is subtle because breathing itself is such an extremely subconscious process. When you mirror and match another person this way, it is almost impossible to detect, yet it is very effective in helping to establish rapport.

While it may sound like an easy thing to do, it will actually take practice to consciously develop this technique. Some good places to subtly develop this skill are when groups of people gather like at a coffee shop, a business meeting or a party.

Speaking

Another technique that can be used to establish rapport with someone else is through your speech patterns, word choices and vocal tones. In order to do this, it is important to first mirror their breathing because without doing that first, you will not be able to speak like someone else if you don't breathe at their pace.

However, once you understand how to do this, it is a powerful tool in directing or facilitating change to create a closer connection with someone.

Physical Posture

The way you walk and stand when you are trying to connect with someone plays a strong role in how whether or not you will be able to establish and/or maintain rapport with them. When you're meeting someone new, always approach with soft movements as you walk toward them but not in a line that moves between their feet but one that is about a foot outside of either of their feet, as though you were intending to walk past them.

When you stand to talk with them, stand in front of them but with your body turned very slightly to one side which is subconsciously recognized as a non-aggressive stance. On the contrary, if you stand directly in front of them so that your centerline matches theirs, your posture could subconsciously be seen as aggressive.

Always make eye contact when you are talking with someone because people who are uncomfortable with making eye contact are often thought of as trying to hide something or even as not being truthful.

Great places to practice your body posture and the way you walk and stand are at work or a social event.

Arms and Hands

Mirroring someone in order to build rapport goes beyond breath, speaking or static posture because most people use movements in order to express themselves. There are movements that are conducive to bringing people closer to you and movements that will drive them farther away. Both forms of movement can be beneficial in developing a connection, but should be used in appropriate situations in order to establish or sustain the rapport that you have developed.

When it comes to hand and arm movements, even though you are mirroring the person with whom you are trying to build rapport, remember that your movements do not have to be to the same degree as theirs. Small arm or hand movements are less threatening than large ones and slow movements are typically more acceptable than large rapid ones.

Remote Rapport

Mirroring is such a powerful way of building rapport that it can even be done with someone from a distance. To demonstrate and fully appreciate the power of mirroring, go to a public place (like a coffee shop or a restaurant where you can sit at a counter) and select someone with whom you would like to establish a connection. Don't approach that person. Instead, get just within their peripheral vision and begin to mirror them from a distance. Sit the way they sit. Breathe at the same pace that they are breathing. If possible, order the same drink that they have and take a sip when they take a sip. Don't attract their attention but subtly keep your attention on them. You will be surprised that before long they will start a conversation with you. They will be drawn to you by your actions.

Some Simple Rules for Establishing and Maintaining Rapport

As you continue using your new abilities for establishing and maintaining rapport, there are a few rules to keep in mind that can help you:

- Keep your facial expressions neutral or identical to that of the person with whom you are building rapport.
- The best facial expression is to very subtly smile with your lips and your eyes.
- Speaking softly but clearly provides better rapport than using a loud, boisterous voice.
- Constant vocal volume is more conducive to rapport than rapidly fluctuating volumes.
- Nodding is always accepted.
- Instead of shaking your head from side to side, just slightly tilt it to show concern.
- Small arm movements are less threatening that large ones.

- Small, slow hand movements are more acceptable than large, rapid ones.

The Messages We All Send

As stated previously, we are all continuously communicating and most of it is done on a non-verbal level. With this understanding you can now begin to comprehend why it is so important that you are careful and aware of the non-verbal messages that you, yourself are continually communicating. Often attempts to build rapport with an individual or a group can be short circuited because of your own non-verbal communication, which the people around you will unconsciously begin to mirror.

Once during a workshop, an instructor received some bad news and even though she tried not to let her anger show, within minutes the class went from engaged and enthusiastic to restless because it took on a very negative tone that was being mirrored from the emotional state of the instructor. The woman had spent a great deal of time getting into rapport with her class, and within minutes that rapport had become negative and was coming back at her.

Remember that your own actions, feeling and moods will affect the actions, feelings and moods of the people around you.

Taking the time to try to establish a connection or build rapport with people will help you to create effective relationships, both on a personal level and on a business level. Building true connections with people is one of the most important processes we have for create a truly happy and successful life.

Resources

1. Emoto, Masaru. *The Hidden Messages in Water.* (Beyond Words Publishing. 2001)
   http://www.life-enthusiast.com/twilight/research.emoto.htm

2. Ducie, Sonia. *Do It Yourself Numerology. (New York: Watkins Publishing. 2007)*

3. Myss, Caroline, Ph.D. *Anatomy of the Spirit.* (New York: Harmony Books, 1996)

For Information and to contact
William D. Horton, Psy.D.
www.drwillhorton.com
941-468-8551

CPSIA information can be obtained
at www.ICGtesting.com
Printed in the USA
FFOW02n1536271115
19080FF